Original Title: Art in the Abstract

Copyright © 2023 Book Fairy Publishing
All rights reserved.

Editors: Theodor Taimla
Autor: Jeannette Viirpuu
ISBN 978-9916-39-387-1

Art in the Abstract

Jeannette Viirpuu

Arcane Aesthetics

Beneath the cloak of twilight's mist,
Veiled secrets clung to alchemist.
Whispers danced in candlelight,
Arcane beauty, shrouded sight.

Ancient scrolls and dusty tomes,
In the lab, where mystery roams.
Elixirs simmering with age,
Letters scribed on history's page.

Transmutations, alkahest,
Silvered vials upon the chest.
The alchemist in silence weaves,
A tapestry that none perceives.

Symbols etched in circles round,
A power soft, yet so profound.
Imbued within the sacred crests,
Are arcane aesthetics, finely dressed.

Muted Motif

In whispers of the ashen sky,
Where muted motifs softly lie.
Through shrouded mists of silent hues,
We find shades of forgotten muse.

The brushstrokes of a world so still,
Where time itself has lost its will.
Canvas pale, devoid of boast,
Embraces every silent ghost.

Strokes of melancholy blend,
Ephemeral, like seasons end.
An artist's touch, so faint and crisp,
On nature's canvas, time has wisp.

Echoes of a subtle draught,
Speaking of a craft unsought.
In every muted pattern seen,
Lies the beauty of a dream serene.

Melody in Monochrome

In shades of grey, the notes escape,
A symphony in twilight's drape.
Each hue withdrawn, the music's pure,
Between each breath, it's the allure.

The keys in solemn contrast play,
Black on white, night meets the day.
In monochrome, melody weaves,
A tapestry that the heart believes.

No spectra needed to enthrall,
Upon my soul, soft shadows fall.
In greyscale tones, the song's embrace,
In every line, a subtle grace.

Harmony in the Haze

Whispers weave within the mist,
Harmony in hazed tryst.
Blurred lines where futures lay,
In fog-bound melodies at play.

From the depth, a chorus rises,
Each note cloaked in sweet surprises.
Blur of sound in dusky air,
Harmonic whispers, everywhere.

In the fog, our senses merge,
As melodies and mists converge.
Ephemeral, the song we hear,
In the haze, it's ever near.

Symphony of Silhouettes

Shadows dance to silent tunes,
Moonlit ballet of dark cocoon.
Silhouettes against the night,
Move in rhythm, out of sight.

Eclipsed figures tell their tale,
As stars above in sky unveil.
Symphony of silent hues,
Within the night, their forms ensue.

A quiet waltz, they sway and turn,
Outlined by what the heavens burn.
Each gesture a note, played unseen,
In the grand symphony of dreams.

Elements of Elation

Beneath the sun's elated stream,
Fields of gold in warmth they gleam.
Air alight with fragrance sweet,
In ardent dance, our hearts do beat.

Waters laugh with pure delight,
Reflecting rays of beaming light.
Skies embrace the lofty heights,
Canvas spread for day's delights.

Fire's passion speaks in glow,
Igniting joy for all below.
Earth responds in silent praise,
In every leaf, the sunlight's blaze.

Silhouette of the Sublime

Upon the peak where heavens kiss the ground,
A shadow cast as twilight sings its tune,
The silhouette of nature's art profound,
The dusk entwines the earth and crescent moon.

A dance of branches swaying with the breeze,
Silent whispers of the wild serene,
A tranquil stance amidst the rustling trees,
The outline of a world so seldom seen.

Majestic mountains etching in the sky,
The silhouette of sublimity dreams,
Where eagles dare in lofty circles fly,
And reality is more than it seems.

The twilight fades to welcome night's embrace,
In silhouettes, the sublime leaves its trace.

Luminosity of the Lost

In the depths where light seldom dwells,
The lost wanderers seek their guiding star,
Luminosity in shadowy spells,
A beacon of hope from realms afar.

The hush of night's velvet canopy spread,
Illuminates souls that time forgot,
The luminescence where the lost have tread,
In the darkest corners, light is sought.

Soft glow of memories that once shone bright,
Faint echoes of laughter in the abyss,
Lost radiance seeking the gift of sight,
Yearning for a touch, a word, a kiss.

Through veils of obscurity, faintly lit,
The lost find luminosity where they sit.

Vibrance of the Void

In emptiness, there echoes a silent cry,
A vibrance veiled by the vast, vacant void,
Colors unseen by the naked eye,
In the nothingness, beauty is deployed.

A space undefined by form or frame,
Breathes life into the void with vibrant hues,
A cosmic canvas with no need for name,
Every shade of nothingness it imbues.

Infinity swirls in spectral dance,
A waltz of wonder in absence of light,
The void vibrates with its own expanse,
Unseen spectra, an invisible sight.

From nothing blooms an energy untold,
The void's vibrance, a marvel to behold.

Elegy of Eclipsed Emotions

In the shadow of a heart grown cold,
Lie eclipsed emotions, buried deep,
Tales of love and loss, never to be told,
Whispered secrets that the soul will keep.

The light of passion once burned so bright,
Now obscured by sorrows of the past,
Feelings fading into the night,
Eclipsed by shadows that forever last.

A silent symphony of inner strife,
Where once vivid hues turned into gray,
The melody of a muted life,
As emotions eclipse and fade away.

In the quietude that darkness brings,
Rest the elegies that the heart sings.

Shades of the Unfathomable

In depths where light dares not to creep,
Mysteries lay in silent keep,
Echoed whispers in the dark,
Elusive shadows leave their mark.

Glimpses of the vast unknown,
Idle thoughts to madness prone,
Beneath the surface tension's brim,
Reality's edges grow dim.

Surreal spectra come alive,
Where thoughts and dreams collide and strive,
An ocean of the abstract thought,
In twilight's grip, the mind is caught.

Shrouded figures in the mind,
Their truest forms we never find,
In endless night they dance and weave,
In shades of the unfathomable we believe.

Frequencies of the Formless

Vibrations stir the silent air,
Unseen, unheard, they're always there,
A symphony sans form or face,
Resounds within the void's embrace.

Waves that dance without a shore,
Palpitations from the core,
Interlacing, pure and raw,
The universe's primal law.

Inaudible to human ear,
Yet in the soul, they resonate clear,
Frequencies of the formless sweep,
In their cadence secrets keep.

They hold the cosmos in their thrall,
In every rise, in every fall,
An unseen force that sculpts the night,
On formless frequencies, we take our flight.

Sketches of the Subconscious

Upon the canvas of the mind,
Untamed visions intertwined,
With gentle strokes and bold intent,
Subconscious sketches are dreamt and spent.

A tapestry of inner sight,
Where colors blend from dark to light,
In dreams these images are born,
From the subconscious they are torn.

The sleeper's brush does not control,
Each dream, a fragment of the whole,
Whispers of the psyche's art,
Reveal the depth of the human heart.

In restless sleep, the truth takes shape,
No escape from the mindscape,
Each sketch, a glimpse within the soul,
A gallery where secrets stroll.

Odes to the Opaque

Opaque the veils that hide the truth,
Mysteries cling to aging youth,
Each shrouded visage, each secret tome,
In shadows' clutch, they find their home.

Unclear, the paths that lie ahead,
With every cautious step we tread,
The opaque maps to futures unknown,
Guide us through the zones unshown.

Eulogies for clarity,
In a world fueled by scarcity,
Odes to that which we cannot see,
The beauty in ambiguity.

We toast to opaque skies above,
Where questions fly on wings of doves,
In the clouded, we seek our place,
And find solace in the opaque grace.

Rhythms in Negative Space

Silent contours play unseen,
Beatless percussion, a soft routine,
Whispers of motion without a trace,
Dance of shadows, negative space.

Void of sound, yet full with vibe,
Absence waltzes, an invisible tribe,
Each empty canvas sings its tune,
Notes in the vacuum, an unheard croon.

Echoes of the void pulse away,
In the unseen, specters sway,
Silhouettes of stillness prance,
In this silent hall, rhythms dance.

Breath of space between each beat,
Pauses where no hearts meet,
Yet in the absence, life resides,
In the hush, a rhythm abides.

Illusions of Intangible Ink

With a quill dipped in dreams unclear,
Scribing on the void, no smear,
Words that dance in the absent ink,
Illusions drawn in the mind's own brink.

Letters of mist, phrases that drift,
Wisps of meaning, they subtly shift,
Script of ghosts that speak to the core,
Tales of the ether that offer more.

Stanzas charmed with the air's caress,
Rhymes that bind to nothingness,
A canvas blank, stories untold,
In the emptiness, wonders unfold.

Verse upon verse in mute recital,
Silent orations, so vital,
In the inkless flow, emotions sink,
An anthology of thoughts, in intangible ink.

Dimensions of the Unseen

Beyond the grasp of the naked eye,
Ancient cosmos whisper and sigh,
Realms unfelt by touch or sight,
The hidden breadth of endless night.

Spaces between the stars unlit,
Realities converge and split,
In layers of the cosmic sheen,
Exist dimensions, yet unseen.

Threads of time weave through the dark,
Uncharted territories, an enigmatic ark,
Realms within realms forever keened,
Universes within the tapestry intertwined.

Mysteries spinning a cosmic dance,
Leaving the tangible in entranced trance,
Every atom pulses with serene,
Unfathomed depths, dimensions unseen.

Harmony in Disarray

In the cacophony of life's grand spree,
Resides a tune that sets hearts free,
Though discord reigns in wild array,
Melodies bloom in the heart of disarray.

Chaos conducts an unscripted choir,
Notes that clash yet strangely inspire,
Out of sync rhythms strut in play,
Crafting beauty in their own way.

Order in the tumult, rhythm in the noise,
In the muddle, a silent poise,
Dissonant pieces, together they sway,
Weaving a symphony of vibrant fray.

Harmony resides where least we seek,
In the mess, it whispers, soft and meek,
Amidst the dissonance, music will stay,
Symphony omnipresent, in disarray.

Fable of Fragments

In slumber's grasp, the pieces flew,
Scattered shards of thoughts so true,
Whispers of a mosaic's dawn,
Dreams in fragmented colors drawn.

Upon the tapestry of mind,
Lost tales of fragments, intertwined,
Within the night, they softly dance,
In morning's light, they still enchance.

A fable spun from break to mend,
Where broken paths to wholeness tend,
Gentle hands the pieces lay,
In life's grand poem, they find their way.

The moral of each shattered part,
Beauty lives in a mended heart,
Whole once more, the story's end,
In fragments found, our souls ascend.

Absence in Aura

A whisper thin, finds space within,
The heart's soft glow begins to dim,
Absence's shade, in silence laid,
A ghostly dance, just faintly made.

In you, the space where light once shone,
Now carries echoes all forlorn,
The aura fades where warmth did dwell,
A hollow curve, an empty shell.

Yet in the void, a subtle grace,
The peace that fills the empty space,
In loss itself, a strange allure,
The silent strength of being pure.

Absence in aura tells its tale,
A silent ship with unseen sail,
Though emptiness may seem to win,
In quietude, the soul takes wing.

Emulsion of the Ether

Swirling in a celestial brew,
Vapors of the cosmos stew,
An emulsion of the ether's cream,
Stirring in the universe's dream.

Stars dip in the milky haze,
Planets blend in astral phase,
Comets streak with fiery tails,
In cosmic soup that never fails.

Nebulas twist in curving streams,
Galaxies spill in silver beams,
The boundaries of heaven blur,
In the mixture of the worlds that were.

Crafting potions in the skies,
Nature's handiwork defies,
Magic in the ether's hold,
The story of the stars, retold.

Spectrum Splinters

In prism's kiss, the colors break,
A spectrum splinters, hues awake,
Refractions spread across the scene,
A tapestry of red to green.

Light divides in arcs so bold,
A secret dance, a story told,
Each band of color finds its place,
Together, yet alone in grace.

From violet whispers to indigo night,
From sapphire seas to emerald light,
Every splinter tells its part,
In the canvas of the heart.

So paint the sky in fragments bright,
Let shades disperse to endless flight,
For in the splinters, truth we find,
In every color, every kind.

Fragments of Fantasy

In realms beyond the waking world we roam,
To touch the skies of an astral dome,
Where unicorns in emerald meadows prance,
And faeries lure the heart into a dance.

Afloat on clouds of silken silver thread,
We navigate the rivers long and dread,
Through whispering woods of ancient, noble trees,
Their leaves tell stories in the twilight breeze.

Enchanted castles locked in time's embrace,
Guard secrets in their stones' cold, stern face,
Spectral knights on endless, silent quest,
Beneath the moon's pale watch they know no rest.

Magic weaves through all that's seen and heard,
In every flower bloom and singing bird,
The fantasy within, a world apart,
Lies fragmented in the dreamer's heart.

Strokes of the Unseen

In hushed and hidden corners of the night,
Where shadows cast by unseen light converge,
Silent figures paint the void with flight,
And on the canvases of dark, emerge.

Their brushstrokes blend the ephemeral themes,
In tones that echo through the hush of time,
Artists of the void, their canvas dreams,
Sketching out existence, sublime.

Evocative shapes in motion swirl,
As they draw the contours of the mind,
Within each stroke, a secret world,
The beauty in the unseen, defined.

The artists vanish with the morning's gleam,
Their masterpiece, a lingering, silent dream.

Pigments of the Imagination

The mind's eye opens, palette in its grasp,
To paint the universe in one bold sweep,
With colors drawn from memories clasp,
In vibrant hues that dreams and visions keep.

Rivers of cerulean thought run deep,
Across the canvas of the inner eye,
Crystalline landscapes where the muses sleep,
And pigments of imagination lie.

Here, the brush dips in a sunset's bleed,
A tapestry of time, it starts to weave,
Blending reality with fantasy's seed,
An intricate dance no one could conceive.

This gallery hung with the unseen,
Showcases the shades of what might have been.

Dance of the Disparate

Upon the stage of variance they twirl,
The opposites with hands so gently clasped,
In rhythm's lock, their differences unfurl,
The dissonance in harmony's grasp.

Discordant melodies begin to rasp,
Transforming swiftly to a sweet accord,
The dissonant, diverse in friendship clasp,
The Dance of the Disparate, struck a chord.

The out-of-tune in symphony unite,
Their steps a blend of chaos and of art,
A pas de deux 'twixt shadow and the light,
Together, spinning worlds apart.

From disarray to beauty they alight,
A dance that shows the sum is greater part.

Chiaroscuro of Chaos

In the woven weft of warring light,
Shadows clash with radiant might,
The tapestry of tumultuous fight,
A chiaroscuro dance ignites.

Whispers thread through braided air,
Chaos blends the dark and fair,
Contrast etched with artist's flair,
Beauty birthed from stark despair.

Ebony ink spills on the scene,
Gold and obsidian intervene,
Deep in the realm of the unseen,
Order lies in the space between.

The palette of the cosmos spills,
A painter's stroke that thrills and chills,
Harmony in discordant frills,
Chaos choreographed with skill.

Gradients of the Ghostly

Spectral mists on fields unfurled,
Haunting the edges of a twilight world,
Gradients of the ghostly swirl,
In this eerie, shrouded burl.

Fading whispers of the yore,
Glide along the moonlit shore,
Haunter's steps on the forest floor,
Trace the light to the lore's core.

Shades of silence, soft and bleak,
Stir the leaves, in whispers speak,
Past and present, they rendezvous,
In the veils of dawn's mild dew.

Ghosts in gradients softly tread,
Across the veil, all fear is shed,
The living dance with the silent dead,
In the space where spirits wed.

Blur of the Boundless

Beyond the reach of time and space,
Where stars and nebulas interlace,
The blur of the boundless gives chase,
Infinity's brush, the cosmos' face.

Eternal depths, a vast expanse,
Celestial seas in their grand dance,
In this ocean, we mere glance,
At the edges of existence's trance.

No walls, no borders in sight,
Boundaries blur in boundless light,
Horizons stretch, to endless height,
A universe's breadth, takes flight.

In the blur, we find our place,
Specks of dust in open space,
In the boundless, our hearts embrace,
The cosmic wonder, time's embrace.

Dalliance with the Dimensionless

Veils of reality softly part,
Opening gateways to the heart,
Dalliance with the dimensionless start,
Drawing back the final curtain's art.

Time's fabric unravels to the touch,
In the void where too is much,
No beginning, end, or such,
In this realm beyond the clutch.

Dance with the formless, pure and wide,
Across the void, in steps untried,
With nothing to hide or to abide,
In dimensionless tides we confide.

Where thoughts and dreams intertwine,
Beyond all concepts of yours and mine,
In silent oneness, we anoint,
The point of points, the joint of joints.

Tones of Transcendence

In whispers of the wind, a quiet plea,
Through rustling leaves, the spirits free.
A chant that rises, breaks the earthly bond,
Transcendent tones, of which we're fond.

Ethereal echoes in sacred space,
Harmonies that time cannot erase.
A symphony of souls in pure ascent,
With every note, more heaven-sent.

Celestial sounds that swirl and spin,
A cosmic dance that dwells within.
A melody that soars and transcends,
In divine chorus, where silence ends.

Immortal hymns in twilight's embrace,
They touch the heart, and leave their trace.
In each refrain, life's essence is found,
In tones of transcendence, we are unbound.

Nebula of Notions

In the womb of space, ideas ignite,
A nebula of notions, birthing light.
Clusters of dreams in astral seas,
Adrift in the cosmic breeze.

Thoughts like comets streaking past,
Glimmering truths that forever last.
A tapestry woven with threads of mind,
Patterns of thought, uniquely designed.

Galactic visions in violet hues,
An interstellar muse to infuse.
Wisps of wonder, a celestial fusion,
In the vastness, a dream's intrusion.

Silent explosions of inspiration's birth,
Stardust settles on the minds of Earth.
From the nebula, our ideas take flight,
In the endless journey of the night.

Crescendo in Color

Strokes of genius on the canvas sky,
A painter's palette where dreams fly high.
Reds blaze forth in passionate sweep,
The canvas alight with secrets to keep.

Yellows burst like the dawn's first light,
A splash of hope in the purest white.
Blues merge into the tranquil sea,
Harmony's hue, soulful and free.

Greens unfurl like spring's first day,
Nature's revival in splendid display.
Purples whisper the dusk's mystique,
The artist's flourish, both bold and chic.

A crescendo in color, life's vivid song,
In every shade, we find where we belong.
The spectrum sings in chromatic cheer,
In this painted symphony, all is clear.

Vestige of the Vague

Amid the mists of memory's lane,
Shadows dance, elusive and fain.
Whispers of past, like veils of lace,
A vestige of the vague, we chase.

Glimpses fleeting, as if through fog,
A spectral bridge from the ephemeral bog.
Moments shrouded in the twilight haze,
Times lost in labyrinthine maze.

Echoes of voices, once loud and clear,
Now hushed, like secrets we hold dear.
With each remnant, our minds engage,
Piecing together the fragmented page.

The vestiges cling like morning dew,
Each drop, a clue that guides us through.
From the deep unknown, wisdom's silhouette,
In the vestige of the vague, past and present met.

Tides of Transformation

In depths of change, the currents shift,
A silent dance, the sands uplift.
Transforming shores with every wave,
Molding the eternal, the sea's brave cave.

Two moons betwixt in silent rage,
Engage the tides that wars assuage.
New lands arise from the ocean's form,
Old rocks erode, as through storms they're torn.

The tides, they rise, and then they fall,
With moonlit whispers, they do enthrall.
From crest to trough, in seamless motion,
The sea's vast tale, a deep devotion.

Within each tide, a tale retold,
A fierce encounter, brave and bold.
The never-cease of change's hand,
Draws futures' face upon the strand.

The Fleeting Fresco

Upon the wall, a story's hue,
A fleeting fresco, bright and new.
Each brushstroke holds a moment's gleam,
An artist's vision, a fleeting dream.

As years pass by the colors fade,
A once-vivid scene to shadows bade.
The walls that bore the artist's heart,
Now silent, watch the paint depart.

Yet in each line, the passion sings,
The fresco's dance of mortal things.
Time may weather, may wash away,
But in the strokes, the soul will stay.

The mural stands, though faint its crest,
A testament of time's own test.
Though fresco fades, the story's told,
In every line, the art grows old.

Paradox of Pigments

A myriad of tints in light's array,
Concealing shades which night displays.
The paradox of pigments bright,
Revealing colors with absence of light.

A canvas shares its vibrant thrall,
Yet in each hue, a shadow's fall.
For every color's vivid life,
An opposing dark, an equal strife.

The crimson love may bleed to black,
As somber notes the void attract.
And golden joy may too recede,
To somber tones, within it seed.

The artist's palette holds the clue,
In every shade, the contrast view.
With light and dark in constant play,
The paradox of pigments stay.

Essence of the Ethereal

Float in realms where dreams are spun,
Ethereal mists that shun the sun.
With whispers light, and touches slight,
The essence courts the edge of night.

A spectral dance across the sky,
Where silence sings, and soft sighs fly.
The ghostly hues of time's soft breath,
In tender grasp, a gentle death.

In airy steps above the ground,
No worldly chains, the spirits bound.
They weave their stories, ether-kissed,
In figments clasped by morning's mist.

Beneath the veils of transient thread,
Lie hidden truths within unsaid.
The essence of what's never seen,
But felt in heart, where it has been.

Shadows of Unseen Brushes

In silence they glide, soft and undefined,
The gentle strokes of night's embrace.
Silhouettes whisper where light can't find,
The touch of mystery's tender grace.

Two lines trace the edge of a slumbering form,
A dance of contrast 'twixt the sheets.
Faint outlines of secrets, a subtle swarm,
Ebbing and flowing in silent retreats.

These unseen brushes, they sweep and they sway,
Crafting visions that day never knows.
In the quiet, our dreams they do softly display,
The hidden artistry that darkness bestows.

The teardrop of moonlight, a brushstroke of chill,
Casting shadows where our thoughts roam.
In the canvas of night, our illusions stand still,
Waiting for dawn to lead them back home.

Palette of Whispering Hues

Tinges speak in hushed tones of light,
Secrets veiled in the colors of dawn.
Each hue a murmur, a delicate sight,
The symphony of the sky being drawn.

Muted whispers of lavender, rose, and gold,
Conversing in strokes across the blue.
The sun, an artist bold and untold,
Painting the morn with dew.

Gentle tints of twilight at the verge of day,
A melange silently speaking of eve.
Crimsons and purples in splendid array,
Their silent discourse we perceive.

In the quiet spectrum that dusk unfurls,
A language of shadows and light.
Our world is brushed in whispering swirls,
A palette of silence so bright.

Canvas of the Cosmos

Stretched across the void, a tapestry wide,
Infinite dark dotted with starlit fire.
Galaxies twirl in an eternal dance,
A celestial painting that does inspire.

Upon this canvas, so vast and so grand,
Constellations tell stories untold.
Brushed by the cosmos, a heavenly hand,
Each star a dot of light, bright and bold.

Nebulas swirl in hues of the night,
With colors that blend at the edge of sight.
Clusters and quasars in boundless array,
Artwork of nature, in splendorous display.

The great black expanse, a backdrop so sheer,
Sets forth the cosmos for all to revere.
A canvas so perfect, so true, and so clear,
In the gallery of the universe, we stand to peer.

Mosaic of the Mindscape

Thoughts tessellate in the mind's quiet room,
A kaleidoscope of ideas that bloom.
Each fragment a piece of the larger scheme,
Picturing life as a waking dream.

Memories glimmer like tiles of glass,
Pieced together in patterns vast.
Reflections of love, shades of the past,
A mosaic where sentiments are amassed.

Dreams and desires are set into place,
Within the mind's intricate embrace.
Vivid visions interlace,
Creating beauty with delicate grace.

Within the gallery of our own making,
Our inner thoughts are ever shaping.
A mindscape of our own undertaking,
The mosaic of our souls, for the waking.

Phantoms of Phosphene

In the darkness, bursts aglow,
Peppered skies in my mind's show.
Phantoms dance behind closed lids,
Dreams set sail, the night forbids.

Colors swirl in silent jest,
Neon dreams upon my quest.
Fleeting figures softly tread,
Whispers of the day now shed.

Jeweled carousel turns free,
As phosphenes dance with glee.
Painting scenes from thoughts unseen,
Ghosts of light in midnight's sheen.

Spectrum's play, the mind's own art,
Invisible from the world apart.
The phantoms waltz in endless streams,
Within the phosphene's silent dreams.

Labyrinth of Lines

Winding paths of ink and lead,
Sketch a maze, thoughts lie unsaid.
Lines entwine in puzzled games,
A journey set by mind's own frames.

Each stroke a choice, a different turn,
In the labyrinth of lines I learn.
Twisting trails of tangled tales,
Where reason shifts and logic pales.

In this maze, my passion burns,
At every corner, fate adjourns.
Endless patterns start to merge,
Where thoughts and fantasy converge.

The pen, my compass through the haze,
Crafts a cryptic, complex blaze.
Lost in art, I find my peace,
The labyrinth's lines offer sweet release.

Radiance of the Residue

The afterglow of moments past,
Shimmering memories that last.
A residue of time's embrace,
Radiant trails we cannot erase.

Echoes of laughter in the hall,
Faint whispers of a lover's call.
The warmth lingers though guests depart,
A tender glow around the heart.

In silent corners, shadows play,
Retelling tales of yesterday.
The residue of joy and strife,
A glowing testament to life.

From embers of a fire gone dim,
New sparks arise, vigorous and prim.
The radiance, a subtle clue,
In every end, beginnings stew.

Enigma of Easel Dreams

Upon my easel dreams take flight,
A canvas bathed in phantom light.
Brushes stroke the silent air,
Pigments whisper secrets rare.

Each hue a riddle to unfold,
A story waiting to be told.
An enigma wrapped in shades of play,
Colors merge in disarray.

Dreams etched on the artist's throne,
A private world, yet not alone.
The easel holds a door ajar,
To universes spun afar.

In strokes of genius dreams are cast,
Each layer deeper than the last.
A tapestry of the mind's own seams,
Woven in the enigma of easel dreams.

The Invisible Ink

Words whispered to the void,

Ephemeral traces on the paper sea,
Invisible ink from the heart's deep sink,
Secrets locked where eyes can't see.

Lines fading as soon as they're born,
Tender thoughts too shy to stay,
They sing in silence, soft and forlorn,
Then like morning mist, they fade away.

The quill dances, light and quick,
In the silence of a writer's lore,
Yet the page stays blank, a clever trick,
A canvas of thoughts, deep at its core.

Only those who dream can truly read,
The tales that shy from the light of day,
In the invisible ink, they plant the seed,
Of stories that live in a hidden ballet.

Ethereal Etchings

Gossamer words in the sky's embrace,

Weaving through the fabric of space,
Ethereal etchings, delicate and fine,
Cosmic canvas, a celestial design.

Strokes of moonlight, brush of stars,
A universe painted in ethereal bars,
Dreams etched on the night's blank slate,
Wishes cast forth, for destiny to navigate.

Skyward strokes from an astral quill,
Where time stands still, the air is chill,
Each line a whisper of the infinite expanse,
A dance of destiny, left to chance.

On this canvas, where dreams take flight,
Etchings glow with an inner light,
Galaxies spun from a gossamer thread,
A tapestry of the unseen, elegantly spread.

The Eclipsed Exhibit

In a gallery cloaked by shadow's veil,

The eclipsed exhibit tells its tale,
A mosaic of moments lost to sight,
Shrouded secrets locked in endless night.

Each piece a whisper of life's elide,
Where colors merge and meanings hide,
A collection of what lies out of view,
The art of absence, a different hue.

Shadows cast upon the lunar glow,
A quiet display where dark dreams flow,
The silenced stories that resonate,
In the quiet halls of a starless fate.

Glimpse the beauty in the hidden arc,
Light and dark entwined to make a mark,
The gallery holds its breath, awaits the day,
When the eclipse yields, revealing hidden display.

Beyond the Bristle

Where strokes transcend the artist's hand,

Ideas sail far from the painted land,
Beyond the bristle, beyond the oil,
In realms where thoughts and dreams recoil.

Canvases whisper of places unseen,
A blend of the real and a touch of dream,
Each hue a voyage beyond the frame,
Wandering freely, untamed, unnamed.

Here, art is more than meets the eye,
It's where the essence of passion lies,
The journey beyond the artist's ken,
In the silence, the paint speaks then.

Deep within the painter's mind,
Truths unravel, unwind, unbind,
Beyond the bristle, they roam free,
In the sacred space where souls can see.

Mirage of the Muse

In desert sands of fervent thought,
A vision of the muse sought,
Where whispers of creation lie,
An oasis in mind's dry sky.

Chasing shadows beneath the sun,
Creative fires, though never done,
She dances just beyond my reach,
In lessons only she can teach.

With each mirage I draw more near,
Her song grows faint, yet ever clear,
Inspiration's teasing dance,
A tempting, elusive trance.

The muse, a mirage of the mind,
Bestows gifts on those who find,
The will to chase what's not in sight,
And turn their darkest dreams to light.

Murmurs of the Motionless

Statues stand in silent wait,
Time's soft whispers to debate,
The murmurs of the motionless,
Tales etched in stone confess.

Marble figures, cold and still,
Watch the world with frozen will,
Eyes that never see the skies,
Yet hold the centuries' cries.

Beneath the quiet of their gaze,
The echoes of the ancient days,
Resound in hushed, immortal tone,
The silent choir turned to stone.

They murmur not for mortal ear,
A language we must learn to hear,
In stillness find the voice of old,
The stories still untold.

Geometry of Genius

Lines intersect in brilliant minds,
Where genius and geometry binds,
Each thought a point in patterns vast,
In the architecture of contrast.

Circles of wisdom perfectly drawn,
Contours of knowledge, early dawn,
Triangles of insight, angles sharp,
Mapping the mind's uncharted part.

Symmetry in ideas, neatly aligned,
Fractal thoughts, complex and twined,
Shapes painted with intellect's hue,
Designs only a genius knew.

In the geometry of the great,
Each equation and curve relate,
In the mind's eye, simple and shrewd,
A universe of thoughts conclude.

Textures of the Intangible

The heart's soft whispers, lightly tread,
Over feelings and words unsaid,
Textures of the intangible heart,
Faint impressions they impart.

Silken strands of thought entwine,
Subtle, yet with strength divine,
The weave of consciousness unwind,
In the fabric of the mind.

Velvet shadows of our doubt,
Satin dreams we can't live without,
Gossamer memories, gently caught,
In the loom of fleeting thought.

Through the tapestry of space,
Past the mind's own gentle lace,
We trace the intangible, feather-light,
A masterpiece beyond our sight.

Patterns of the Profound

Whispers of wisdom in winds sway,
Patterns profound in the soul's clay.
Intricate webs of fate are spun,
Journey's begun with the morning sun.

Subtle are the strokes of life's art,
Each hue imparts a vital part.
In chaos and order, truth is found,
Silent and sound, profound is crowned.

Through the labyrinth, seekers tread,
Bearing threads of the words unsaid.
Mysteries dance in daylight's blind,
In patterns entwined, seekers find.

Stars above in harmony move,
Guiding the groove of the cosmos' loom.
Galaxies spin, a tapestry,
In the patterns of infinity.

The Abstract Affair

In splashes of colors unseen,
Abstract thoughts float in a dream.
Ideas meld in strange ballet,
Silhouettes of grey in light's beam.

Emotion's palette rich and broad,
Strokes of genius, quirky and odd.
Canvas of mind, the heart's affair,
Abstracted care fills the quad.

Patterns emerge from the chaos,
Concepts engage us, emboss.
Lines intersect in a soft flare,
Abstract affair with no loss.

Masterpieces brew 'neath the skin,
Thought's vast ocean, tumble and spin.
Art from the heart, wildly free,
An abstract spree, begins within.

Nocturne of Nuances

Moonlit whispers 'cross the sky's face,
Nuances trace night's soft embrace.
Zephyrs hum a lullaby tune,
Stars commune in the darkened space.

Velvet shadows weave through the trees,
Night's ballet teases the breeze.
Crescent glow, a silvery lance,
In this dance of nuances.

Whispers veil the nocturne's heart,
Subtle art from daylight apart.
Every shade a hidden chance,
In elegance, the nuances.

Dreams unfurl like petals at night,
In the light of the moon's soft bite.
Mysteries, the soul's romance,
Under the trance of nuanced light.

Evocation of the Ecliptic

Sun and moon in celestial chase,
Ecliptic's grace in cosmic space.
Shadows blend in an astral kiss,
Ephemeral bliss in solar bliss.

Planets align in silent creed,
Ecliptic's deed, they all accede.
Orbits cross in an arc's embrace,
Space's own lace, in sky's broad place.

Eclipse unveils the curtain's edge,
Time and light wed on the ledge.
Cosmic dance of dark and light,
Ecliptic's night and day fight.

Stars etch their paths in heaven's dome,
Through the loam of the ether's home.
Evoked in orbits' cryptic glyph,
Ecliptic's myth forever roams.

Alchemy of Absence

In the void where love once dwelled,
A flame doused by the winds of time,
Elusive touch, a phantom's hymn,
Cherished moments now resigned.

Two shadows cast by single light,
Dances of memory soft and faint,
An alchemist stirs the quiet night,
Trying to paint what picture can't.

Whispers of the heart's retreat,
In spaces where the echoes call,
Gold from lead, a feat so sweet,
Yet heavy in the heart it falls.

Absence crafts its secret lore,
Transforming all it ever kissed,
The more it takes, it gives much more,
In the tender alchemy of missed.

Reverie in Relief

In quietude, the mind takes flight,
Beyond the gloom, above the strife,
Dreams blossom in the hush of night,
Brushing color on the canvas of life.

A symphony played by the silent mind,
Notes unseen lifting the veils of grief,
It's here in stillness, new paths we find,
And bathe our souls in sweet relief.

The heavy heart, like a saturated cloud,
Finds in repose, a place to release,
A reverie wrapped in a silver shroud,
A respite that molds our inner peace.

So close your eyes, let tranquility be found,
In the silent vault of your sacred belief,
For it is in pause, our hopes are unbound,
Bathing us softly in reverie's relief.

Illusive Interlude

In the pause between breath and sigh,
A fleeting glimpse of worlds unseen,
An interlude where dreams may fly,
On quiet wings, through realms of green.

The ticking clock holds its hands with care,
Allowing time a moment's respite,
In the calm, we glide in the airy stair,
With phantom steps, light as the night.

Echoes of a life not quite our own,
Dancing figments of an ethereal masquerade,
We play our parts in the unknown,
Until reality's sharp edge begins to fade.

Illusive pause, a delicacy so rare,
A blink, and the magic comes undone,
But in that second, we travelled where,
Our hearts danced freely, in unison.

The Shapeless Symphony

In the quiet orchestra of the formless realm,
Instruments of silence play a noteless tune,
Their cadence flows like a helmed helm,
Invisible waves beneath the moon.

A symphony not heard, but deeply felt,
The pulse of the world in a silent roar,
Where shapeless melodies make hearts melt,
In a dance of elements, core to core.

Is it the wind that hums through the trees?
Or the river's run that sings to stones?
It's the quiet choir of nature's tease,
In every rustle, in all the undertones.

Invisible threads that weave through the air,
Connect every life, play every part,
In this shapeless symphony, all is fair,
For the music lives deep within the heart.

Silent Strokes of the Mind

Within the quiet corners, thought does wind,
A brush that paints where silence is confined.
Ideas dance in the hush of unseen art,
Mind's canvas holds the strokes that never part.

Subtle shades of might-have-beens intertwine,
Gentle lines of whispers form a design.
Memories flicker, a delicate find,
In soft-spoken hues, they're gently outlined.

Dreams etch in mute, their vibrancy is blind,
Each silent stroke a piece of the entwined.
In contemplation's gallery, unsigned,
The mind's masterpieces are thus defined.

Secret galleries of thoughts, so aligned,
In the silence, our deepest selves are mined.
Ponderings traced without a sound, enshrined,
In the quiet, life's sketches are refined.

Echoes of Invisible Brushes

Echos linger from strokes that do not show,
Invisible artistry's soft glow.
The canvas breathes with what the heart does know,
A painting felt, not seen, its hidden flow.

Tender emotions, outlined with care,
Each stroke is an echo filling the air.
Absence of color, yet fully there,
Invisible masterpiece drawn with flare.

Inaudible the brush may seem,
Yet its echo resonates in a dream.
The painter's quiet, a silent scream,
On a canvas where the unseen gleams.

Whispers of a hand that paints unseen,
The heart knows where the brush has been.
In the echo, the colors convene,
In the silence, a hidden scene.

Palette of Dreams Unseen

In the realm of the slumbering, colors blend,
Unseen palette where dreams and reality mend.
Each hue a wish, in soft clandestine streams,
Crafting a tapestry out of moonbeams.

Shades of hope merge with tints of deep desire,
Glistening in the dark, like stars afire.
Dreams are painted where the eyes can't gaze,
On a canvas where night secrets laze.

Whispers of sleep weave through the obscure,
Blends and contours, a vision so pure.
Emotions dabbed on a spectral lure,
In dreams, life's palette remains demure.

Dusky strokes of a slumber's charming scene,
Crafting fantasies, soft and serene.
In the quiet night, they're felt, not seen,
A world of hues, in the somnolent sheen.

Chromatic Whispers

Whispers in hues, softly they speak,
Of feelings too tender, of moods so meek.
Colors converse in a spectrum discreet,
Telling tales in shades that never deplete.

A murmur of violet, a sigh of blue,
Each chromatic whisper feels fresh and new.
Hushed tones tell stories without ado,
In the quiet, a vivid tableau grew.

Muffled are the voices of the unsaid,
Yet in vivid whispers, their stories spread.
In the palette of silence, emotions are read,
A canvas of whispers, eloquently led.

Subdued symphony of the unsung,
Each color speaks with a silent tongue.
The whispers of hues softly among,
The canvased silence, forever young.

www.ingramcontent.com/pod-product-compliance
Lightning Source LLC
LaVergne TN
LVHW020421070526
838199LV00003B/226